COMPLINE

KARYN M. BRUCE

ISBN: 9798390834435
Editors: Matthew Lippman, Richard Messer
Book Cover Design and Interior Format: Melissa Stevens,
www.theillustratedauthor.com

Cover photo taken by Karyn M. Bruce. Permission to use given by the artist and sculptor of Sacred Space: The Seven Dancing Women at the Cove, Atlantis, Antonius Roberts.

pg. 78 photo taken by Karyn M. Bruce. Permission to use given by the artist and sculptor of Sacred Space: The Seven Dancing Women at the Cove, Atlantis, Antonius Roberts.

Photographs used in this book were taken by the author and are the sole property of the author. The rocks, leaves, etc. have not been placed for the photos. They are where they were found by the author.

TABLE OF CONTENTS

PRAYER

COMPLETORIUM

"This is a powerful book. It's beautiful how Karyn Bruce shows the dross, the everyday details of physical life as a part of spirituality…an insight into the burdens people carry. I love the wonderful details, the real sensations the author evokes with her images. I hope this book reaches those who need to hear its truths and experience her telling the way it is for her so beautifully."

~Richard Messer~
Murder in the Family, A Life on Earth, Dark Healing

"Inside Compline is the very soul of the author on display - a fearless exhibition of love, loss, and friendship. Also ever-present are themes of mortality and questions of faith which are balanced beautifully through the eyes of humor and heartache. Karyn Bruce bravely refuses to lay the past to rest, and not for fear of sacrificing the present, but rather to stockpile hope for the future. She paints here an honest and poignant portrait of faith and prayer in the images of all that is alive. It's beautiful. It made me cry."

~B. T. Keaton~
Transference

In her poems, she brings us, perhaps, to a new way to see God, and she speaks to the reader in carefully crafted word images that makes each view fresh, almost three-dimensional, while maintaining depth and clarity of her intent. The images are simple, but they are loud.

~Phyllis Nye~
free-lance writer, poet, and a columnist for "Guest Columns" in the Marshall, Michigan, newspaper.

ACKNOWLEDGEMENTS

Coneflower Café , The Ann Arbor Review, Pensive,
The Halcyone – Her Words,
Dark Moon Lilith, Talking River Review, A Joyful Noise.

IN GRATITUDE

I would like to thank my family for all of their love and support–**Steve**, my husband; **Cathy**, my daughter; **Danny**, my son-in-law; **David**, my step-son; and **Anna Grace**, my granddaughter. You all are my rock and I love you so much. I am grateful every day that you are in my life.

I would also like to thank my very best-friends-for-life: **Barbara Dahnke, Judy Brown, and Phyllis Nye**. The three of you have been by my side for a very long time, and I am deeply blessed to have you in my life. You might not always understand me or what I write, but you lend an ear, a smile, a tissue, a phone call, a text, and you never let me give up on *me*.

Matthew Lippman, I thank you for your time, patience, honesty, and all of the encouragement that you have given me over the past years. You are a master mentor and poet, and I am grateful to you.

Another poet and mentor I'd like to thank is **Richard Messer**. Your guidance as my BFA college professor has brought me to where I am today and I'm so glad in so many ways that you are my friend.

I also thank **Melissa Stevens**, *The Illustrated Author*, for her time and patience in illustrating this book. She is artistic and creative beyond measure.

There is another group of people who I wish to thank, and they are the "sisters" I lived with in the convent after high school. I found my calling there, though I was asked to leave, but your advice, caring, prayers and sisterhood has been with me all these years: **Morreece Cook, Cynthia Sartor, Susan Pocock, Denise Richmond, and Joan** (who left us too soon). And thank you to those who have been in my life and heart for a very long time, **Mary Hillman, Rev. Maryjane Peck, Donna Monahan, Sharyn Snyder, Cindy Loser, Marjorie Waterman, Nancy Pruitt Redmond, Jesse,** and **Mary Ann**. Your love, guidance, encouragement, and laughter are always with me.

I would also like to thank a man who was willing to help a stranger find sea glass, drive her anywhere she wanted to go on Paradise Island, and to deliver a letter to the sculptor of The Sacred Place for her. Thank you, **Clement Russel**.

It is with the greatest gratitude that I wish to thank **Mr. Antonius Roberts** for granting me permission to use my photographs of his creation, Sacred Space: The Seven Dancing Women at the Cove, Atlantis for this book. They speak the silence of God, in the prayers of one's soul.

Most of all, thank you, **Sister Francis Marie Gerhard, RSM**.

PREFACE

In *Compline*, Karyn Bruce tends the threshold between day's end and the deep quiet of night. Her poems inhabit spaces where light fades—stained glass dimming after Sunday Mass, the shoreline emptied of lovers, the forest floor alive with unseen breath—and listen for what lingers when human presence recedes. These are places where prayer, like tidewater, leaves its residue long after the congregation or the sun has gone. Bruce's voice is contemplative but unafraid of shadow, attending to the quiet hum beneath stillness, the whispers that continue when the world appears to have fallen silent.

Her work returns again and again to the charged moment of transition, when something departs and something else, unseen, takes its place. The collapsing sandcastles and scurrying crabs in one poem are as present and vivid as the organ closed after Mass, the Hail Mary's murmuring through incensed emptiness. Bruce's imagery dissolves boundaries between the sacred and the natural, between ritual and erosion, until both seem part of the same slow liturgy. In her hands, the retreating ocean and the echoing nave speak in a shared language of reverence, absence, and renewal.

Yet *Compline* is not simply a collection of quiet meditations. It also listens to the louder silences—the ones filled with grief, fear, and urgency. In "So Loudly," Bruce's voice rises into the communal register of streets and voices, mourning and injustice, where silence becomes suffocating rather than serene. These moments remind us that the hour of compline, the final prayer before rest, is not always gentle; it can also be an hour of reckoning, where darkness demands we name what we would rather not see.

In these poems, evening is not the end but a kind of turning, a time when the boundaries between prayer and ocean tide, between shadow and skin, between mourning and morning, grow porous. Bruce writes with a sensibility attuned to both the smallest shifts in light and the grandest, loudest silences. *Compline* invites us to linger there—to listen as the last colors of the day smash against the clouds, to breathe in the hush of an emptied church, and to feel, in the hum of the darkness, that what is dying and what is being born are always present together.

This is a book of the heart. It's generous. It's accessible and enveloping. There is so much tenderness, sadness, and joy bouncing off of these poems that we 'see' the speaker as an extension of ourselves. Her ability to take the specific and make it universal is the light from the darkness, the glimmer out of the shadow. Read this book at night, during the day, in the middle space between morning and afternoon. It's a book for all time that transcends time itself.

Matthew Lippman – author of *We Are All Sleeping With Our Sneakers On*

COMPLINE

The ancient office of Compline derives its name from a Latin word meaning completion, "completorium." It is above all a service of quietness and reflection before rest at the end of the day.

COMPLINE

Eyes closed. Fingers intertwined.
We learn the words to our first prayer. "Now I lay me down to sleep."
We are two, or three, or four. It is bedtime, and we are kneeling
beside our bed, practicing to be holy to please our parents,
our grandparents, our aunts and uncles, our brothers and sisters.
We memorize every word and remember our "God blesses,"
and we grow up believing that all our prayers will be answered.

After Sunday Masses, the church is empty,
lights dimmed, the organ closed. In the crouching shadows,
the stained glass windows lose the sunlight that had poured in
during the Consecration when the bread and wine became Jesus
and we lined up to refill ourselves with holiness.
And then we go home.

But prayers never leave. They are always there,
whispering up and over the pews, words murmuring
until the incensed emptiness reverberates the "Hail Mary's",
"Our Fathers", the "Act of Contrition." Like ghosts wafting
up and over the statutes of saints, the prayers
are haunting and loud and shouting "*please* God." The prayers,
echoing in and out of the vestibule and confessionals and choir loft.
A thousand voices petitioning, pleading, beseeching day and night.
Even when they are mumbled by the quiet, old women who come to clean
every Wednesday, the words bang inside the chancery and up and around

the painted saints on the walls, every prayer and psalm
colliding into the altar, splashing into the holy water and dripping
from abandoned rosaries. The prayers are always there, fingerprinting
the space like sticky notes on a refrigerator.

I get a headache from the noise and I worry about God.
There is no prayer for that.

VIGIL

2

IN THIS ROOM
WHERE SHE NO LONGER IS

They have put my mother's body
inside a black, plastic bag.
I watched them zip her up, watched them
push the gurney down the hall.
The men in black suits took her body away.

But I cannot leave this room.
Her last words are somewhere
pressing against the white walls
or clinging to the rain-stained windows.
Somewhere in this room
her last thought is fading into the white curtains.
Her last breath is disappearing into the white sheets.

I see the only sound I do not hear.
A drop of blood. Still red. On the white pillow.

AUTUMN

When I was a child
Autumn scented the air
with chilling winds
and a rainbow of colors
that made more sense to me
than the blues, greens, purples
my friends would draw
on their papers at school
because I liked the smell
of scarlet and gold
and the russet leaves
already brittle in their spinning
around my Buster Browns
and I felt adopted, secreted,
amused by the whisperings
that swirled on the sidewalks
where I longed for the stain
of bittersweet,
dying the way it would,
weaving its way inside me
like the dreams of little old ladies
dressed in vintage poems and
yellowed lace, crocheted into
another September.

WANDERING INTO A SAGINAW CEMETERY THAT AFTERNOON

For an old poet

we searched for Roethke's grave all afternoon,
you needing to sift through dirt and overgrowth
to enter, somehow, his greenhouse hermitage
that place where his large, cumbersome hands
potted the black, wet wombs,
forcing tiny shoots up from their darkness.
I watched you bend down
to brush away one leaf, then another,
moving as a shadow across these weather-worn markers
like one of the small creatures that hunk of a man
mused into a poem.

I could not have known then or understood
how roots appear, then wisps almost invisible,
pushing, pulling, yet each moment a painful struggle
a rhythm so close to death
one dare not breathe too closely, too far away.

I remained distanced
watching you, wandering through words and phrases
each year offering some small piece of a cutting, a poem
for this man who waltzed his way across a greenhouse floor
and gave back life to that which might have never survived if untended.

And I, who can now feel the veins of small stems
suck water from autumn rain, bulge up and over thick, hardened dirt,
wonder if you still search old notebooks for poems once saved,
as Roethke there, nudging roots and nubs, a word or phrase buried there,
knowing, as he knew, *nothing gives up life*.

SACRIFICE
THE ACT OF OFFERING A DEITY
SOMETHING PRECIOUS

When I was eight years old, I stopped telling people
how I met Jesus. It was a memory I talked about all the time
when I was younger, younger than five. My Aunt Florence
hadn't taken me to Bible school yet, and my mother hadn't
taught me how to pray "Now I Lay Me Down to Sleep."
But I knew Jesus. I mean. I. knew. Jesus.

We all grow up remembering the first time we rode a bike
or the first time we went to school.
And there I was playing with my dolls, telling my parents
that before I was born, I tried to save Jesus.
Before I was born, I was a little angel with white wings
beside Jesus, hanging from a cross.
Before I was born, I saw scary people throwing garbage
yelling and screaming at Jesus, hanging from a cross.
Before I was born, I flew in front of Jesus and yelled back
at the scary people throwing garbage at Him hanging from a cross.
My parents made me stop telling my story.
They told me I must have dreamt it. And I just shook my head.
I knew Jesus. And I had tried to save Him.

8

We all grow up with messy parts in our lives. Moments we remember
when we were left alone, when we were afraid, when we were angry, even hateful.
We all have secrets we have had to hide to keep them safe, or to keep ourselves safe.
I never told my friends. I never told my teachers.
Even when I went to Catechism classes, I never told the nuns.

But in my heart I knew it had to be true.
When I was screaming in the back seat of my mother's car
as she swerved and weaved us down the road, I remembered.
When my father was beating on my mother, I remembered.
When I entered the convent, I remembered, even though
the nuns thought I had nothing to offer Jesus.

We lose our memories as we grow older. We forget times and places and words.
Once upon a time, there was a little girl who remembered trying to save Jesus.
And then she was born.

MYSTERIOUSLY RAVISHING

I want to be old and wrinkled like trees who have swished their leaves
into a thousand seasons. I want to be cracked and gnarly like corn stalks
across the Michigan fields in September, even October before the snows fall.
I like old. Phones with plug-in cords on tables, black-and-white lace-up
saddle shoes. Penny Loafers. I wore Buster Brown shoes until I was seven or eight.
And they were brown. Old. Like 33 1/3 records. Ella Fitzgerald and Billy Holiday.
Benny Goodman. Lawrence Welk. I love hats – low, slanted, netted, flowered
like every woman who lived in the 30s and 40s. And I think paper dolls
are the most fun to play with, especially if you make your own paper clothes,
which I did in my 6th grade classroom and never got caught.

I want to be old and stylish like Gretta Garbo, mysteriously ravishing.
Like Shirley Temple, tap-dancing her way across Broadway stages. Old.
Like black-and-white movies. "The Mummy's Hand" and "The Mummy's Ghost."
Bella Lugosi in the "Night of Terror" with organ music and horrible make-up that
my first boyfriend and I laughed about every Saturday on the phone.

I love old. Not relic. Or antique. Anything with yellowed lace and pearls.
And Drive-In movie theaters with popcorn and steamed-up windows. Old like
crocheted doilies. I love the smell of old. The cobwebs in an attic. My grandmother's
house. Not senile. Not forgotten. Old like songs my father sang to me. I want to be old
like hand-rolled snowmen and home-made hot chocolate. Like '57 Chevy's
and cruisin' the gut. Hot dog stands and Down-Towns. Rock 'n Roll '45s.
Old. Like fading photographs hanging on living room walls. Old.
Like shadows. In churches.

DON'T KILL THE IGUANA

We spent the morning wandering around the park adjacent to the river.
We had forgotten the dried-up bread we had set out on the kitchen counter
for the turtles, which actually was always eaten by the catfish,
so we walked through the overhang of tree branches, greens and browns
dangling over us like a delirious ratted mess of teenage hair from the 80s.
But it was quiet, except for our footsteps and whispers on the dirt path.
There were no birds. Neither one of us knew why.
It was Sunday, and this is how we prayed.

It's how the iguanas looked to us, statues almost, there on the wet grassy banks,
in groups of three. Twelve in all. Like the Apostles. Or prayer service.
They were quiet there, watching us. Their big eyes still. Unblinking.
I wanted to stay, sit with them, watch them ever-so-slowly return to the river,
dunk themselves in, and then dry in the sun on the banks,
with their bright greens and reds and oranges and purples glistening,
like someone now free from sin. An echo. Like a last Amen.

But my husband, now so many steps away, was in a hurry. We were headed
to Barnes and Noble to buy books. Real books. The ones that rest
in your hands, and have pages that turn and get used and fingerprinted.
And smell like. Books. A trip we had not taken in over a year.
I had read twenty-six books during that first year of the Pandemic,
the electronic kind that need batteries charged right in the middle of the best part
of any chapter. But it was Sunday. And there were these iguanas
that filled my mind. With their eyes.

On the way to the bookstore I was reading a book about Mr. Rogers.
The man with sweaters and stories and neighbors.
I was in the middle of the chapter about "silence" and how he had a gift
for "driving slow," creating pockets of quiet moments for the children
who watched him on television. He said it was good for their souls
to take their time. Like the iguanas at the park. Watching.

As we were going through what we called "church drive," because
there were so many churches along that route and the music and song
drifted up and over colliding into each other's words and prayers.
I saw a little iguana, dressed up in Sunday green, crossing the street
right there in front of our car. I screamed, "Don't kill the iguana" to my husband
who didn't slow down, but quickly swerved the car to the left.
It was only a palm frond, he said. I closed my eyes, while my mind
was screaming again and again "There are no palm trees here."

I never looked back, and on our return trip home with our books,
I kept reading about Mr. Rogers as slowly as I could, so I wouldn't see
that small creature, lifeless on the road. The churches' music still swayed
through the air, voices louder and louder, in praise and majesty.
I thought about Jesus, wondering if he shouted out, "Don't kill the messenger"
there, nailed to the cross, waiting to die, while his mother's hands held her tears.

14

IN THE ABSENCE OF BREATH

We have a dove sitting outside in our tree.
A white dove we have never seen before.
She cocks her head when I creep out from the kitchen
to speak to her, as if she knows what I am saying
or trying to. The rain has not detoured her from her branch
although I wish I could give her shelter.

It's been raining for weeks now. Drops of water plummet down like rocks.
Day and night, the streets are flooded and our bird feeders
are pools of water and floating bird seed. She prefers the seeds
that fall to the ground, the ones the blue jays and pigeons
and cardinals and squirrels pitch out onto the grass.
We have yet to see her sitting in the bowl that swings
from the tree, and once she finds a branch she likes
she sits gracefully and watches the other birds, flapping
and diving down for more and more food. She sits. Watching.

For days now, she has not flown away. She has not
been afraid when I slowly move toward her, stand not too close
or not too far. She is soundless, understanding rain better
than I do, tucking her head beneath her white feathers until
there is a lull in the pounding drops that slip off her body,
and she peeks out into the bands of sunlight.
I have never known such quiet, and I hold my breath
lest I disturb the whisperings of God.

BETTY JO'S KITTEN DIED IN THE CELLAR

For Richard, who appreciates Hemingway

In the old Hemingway House
the wooden fans turn slowly enough to arouse the scent
of stale tobacco & long mornings
when voices crawled across the unfinished manuscripts.

The Spanish bedrooms are painted
with musty sunsets & colors of the cheapest wine,
while ragged rugs lay casually across the wooden floors
as if someone had just shuffled across them.

I come here to this house again & again
to walk along the tiled porches like the six-toed cat
who ignores the trespassers & memorized speeches
of tour guides & exuberant readers of your work.

I was twelve when I found out you were dead,
long before I knew you were alive.
From you I learned the word "suicide"
& even then, I thought it was a waste of vocabulary.

My mother's friend, Josephine, had given me your
To Have and Have Not, but the pages had yellowed,
& the book was dusty,
& the word "death" crept up my fingers as I read.

Years later, I would struggle through your imagination,
find it empty & unresolved with the hollowness
of the last moment in *The Sun Also Rises*.
As I sat in that Ohio college classroom,
filled with students who hung on your every word,
I often wondered if it was me or your writing
that prevented me from knowing that Georgette,
the character everyone admired the most, was a prostitute.

I do not want to be remembered as I remember you,
as I walk into each garden, near the pool,
& rest in the summer's chair,
while inside the bed of philodendron
golden eyes fill with shadows,
your cats living as if nothing has changed.

I sit beneath the umbrella leaves
all through the stickiness of this afternoon
& think about Betty Jo,
a cat whose kitten died in the cellar
& the poem I will write to honor her.

FOR SUSAN,
WHEREVER GOD CAN FIND HER

I joined the convent, entered the eternal space of spiritual echoes,
Gregorian chants, Grand Silence, a Bible. And Susan. The witty-magical-
blonde-haired-daringly-uninhibited postulant who twisted my soul, who
took my hand for two years and led me down the path of breaking rules
and bending prayers.

She was my midnight partner whose friends smuggled cigarettes to us
in the dead of night, who found hiding places where we could talk, cry,
laugh, without being caught. She crept into my heart and kept me safe
and alive from the confines of obedience. We could not pass each other
in the hallways without biting our lips and praying to God to keep us quiet.

We both left the convent, went our separate ways. I visited her at college,
spent long nights gossiping, smoking in her dorm room. We were "seculars"
now, free to be young women of the world. Short skirts, boyfriends.
She would be my best friend through it all. We would grow old and have
jobs, husbands, children. But, no one had taken her dream away from her.
She had left the convent on her own, while the nuns had sent me home.

She never wrote to me to say goodbye when she later entered the cloistered hallways
of a New York convent where her own sister was bleeding out her prayers
for the poor in a darkened chapel. Susan, my partner in crime, the comedian
of my spirituality, the sassy girl of the novitiate would slip away behind
cloistered convent walls and disappear into the whispers of old nuns
in endless hours of lauds, vespers, compline. To Jesus.
I didn't understand why she would empty her soul there.
For fifty years, I have wondered who has made God laugh.

I REMEMBER

I would watch her
brushing her hair into the perfect Page-boy
and applying lipstick and rouge before leaving for work.
She would smile down at me, then kiss me on the cheek.
I left the ruby-red stain on all day long,
peeking into the mirror every once in awhile
to make sure it was still there.

She only shopped at Jacobson's, which was
the most expensive clothing store in town.
Walking in, holding tightly to her hand,
I always felt the same way I did when I saw
glamorous Claudette Colbert in the movies I watched,
strolling into Tiffany's or Macy's, all glitzed and fabulous,
the way my mom looked when we walked into Jacobson's
and all eyes were on her.

I remember the jewelry counter the most,
the gold and silver charms that hung like Christmas decorations
and had moving parts, especially the carousel with tiny horses
that went around and around. I had never owned a charm bracelet,
but oh! how I dreamed about having one! Coming into Jacobson's
by myself, my mother's daughter, and asking the clerk to show me
the newest, shiniest charm. And then watching the bracelet
hang on my wrist, the charm perfectly displayed, twinkly and expensive.
It was like a holiday, every time we walked down the isle
to the women's clothes. She and I. Those suave skirts and silk blouses,
the pearly-diamond-feathery hats like Joan Crawford wore.

My first credit card was from Jacobson's,
a piece of plastic that could buy me anything up to $50.
I never wore red lipstick, or suits with shoulder-pads. Not then.
I hardly ever wore high heels or the silkiest of nylons.
And I never bought a charm bracelet
or even the carousal charm with the dancing horses.
All grown up, I didn't dress to "the nines" or paint my nails.
I used to pretend she was there with me, and together we would go
to the clothes she would have bought. And I'd try them on,
pretending her approval. She never saw the woman-version-of-me.
The one who still loves old timey black-and-white 1940 movies,
songs by Peggy Lee, and a store called Jacobson's
where all the best memories were always in the back, just off to the right.

BEFORE THE DEATH
OF DONALD HALL
AFTER THE DEATH OF JANE

Would you let me in if I showed you my latest poem
about trees and rivers that shimmer in morning daylight,
while all the lines are drifting across the page like fish
beneath the green shiny surface,
flipping their tails and gurgling their songs?
I want to come in, although I have no right to be here.
I have no right to smell the emptiness of the upstairs bedroom
where she slept, or touch the sunlight that falls
on the few tangled hairs left in her hairbrush.
But I want to come in and sit in the rocking chair there by the fireplace
and walk with Dog out into the fields of summer flowers buried now in winter snow.
I want to go out to the barn and watch the moon rise above my head
while I linger, watching my breath slip into the night of a poem.

I want to be here, beside the windowsill, though I should not,
to watch cardinals perch and build nests on the weathered branches
or by the cat as she washes herself on the linoleum floor.
I have dreamt of the fields in autumn, there where apples drop from trees
and the smell of cinnamon muffins warm the hours long into afternoons.
I want to slip into her words, searching for the shadows she has left behind.

I have no right to be here while you weave the echoes of her absence
across Eagle Pond, gather her fingerprints from coffee mugs
and the butter knife that will never be washed again.
Her breath. On the poem. The one she must have left you to read. After.

I did not know her. I have no right to be here,
and I will leave with this poem while you walk Dog
as he still searches the fields for her along the worn-out path
to the church. I should not be here.
There are these spaces, you know. I hear them. between words.

WHAT CHILDREN BELIEVE

They have turned into wisps that now do not know
they must let the wind's breath carry them away.
I do not know how many times I plucked a dandelion
from the ground, brown and wrinkled, and lifted it up
to blow the tiny "angels" out into the sky,
always wishing, *always wishing* for someone to rescue me,
believing time after time, and waiting, just waiting, until
my parents turned into parents and my home no longer
their battleground.

But, wishes are death traps, shriveled up,
stuck in trees or the last moment before sleep ends.
They are fairy tales for fairies that do not live. The truth is
nothing happens except the white-feathered seeds twirl up
and land on autumn-scorched fields to birth again the lies
meant for left-over children. But it's a lovely thought,
taking scared and lonely children away from their darkness
and sending them to God.

WHILE SHE WAITS

For M & M

When I think of her, I think about all the adventures we have been on.
The driving through the country to take her then eight-year-old son
to summer camp. The many times we drove for hours to see
my granddaughter, up north, then just a toddler. Talking the hours
into more hours. How many times we sat at her kitchen table,
drinking rum and coke, those catch-up summer visits in person,
laughing for hours about boyfriends or lovers or finally-divorced-husbands.

When Covid hit, the visits stopped, but we spent hours on the phone.
Just words away. It was easy then, to be close. to be friends,
sequestered from the death all around us, while snowstorms pelted
her daytimes and sunshine burned through mine.

We have spent years like this. Waiting. Phoning. Even when Covid was curtailed
and vaccines and booster shots were free. I needed surgery. Her husband
needed her. We talked less as we acquainted ourselves with an environment
of maybes. And memories. We have been sisters, weaving moments
through moments while I crocheted blankets, and she sat by her husband
wondering how many months he would have left as he passed
through each emergency room visit, oxygen tank in tow. The hours she sat,
watching him breathe. We told each other everything, wondering if
there was something forgotten. Something we missed. We called less,
texted more as the months turned into winters that brought delayed springs for her.
Sunny days and hurricanes for me. Years and years for both of us in echoes.

I read books. She read more books. We both read *The Women's Murder Club.*
We watched TV though vastly different shows. And not together.
There was always a story or two about our children, struggling through
the years we had already passed. And now our grandchildren in school.
We muttered *oy veys*, though I am not Jewish, and we laughed. We talked
our way through every season of dogs and cats. Sometimes a ground hog
thrown in for humor.

She tells me that her husband can play cards now, have dinner with the neighbors.
He is driving again, sometimes. In the darkening evenings, they sit and sleep
in the lounge chairs, side-by-side in their living room through
hours and hours of taped TV shows, their dog lounged between them.

We share everything while nothing is shared, and memories shared are fading.
We do not discuss prayers, but I send mine to God each day, not knowing if
I should pray for a miracle or a quiet death. For him. Unable to tell her over the phone.
If she were here. If I were there. We both know that will not happen.
There is no room for me at her house as it gathers more and more last moments.
I speak of coming. After. She does not reply. I wonder if I will. I do not ask again.

We keep gathering more moments like the leaves that fall from her Walnut trees.
Or the walnuts that fall over the leaves each year and the hours it takes her to
bag them up. They are up at dawn, watching deer and rabbits from their kitchen
window. Their cat does his best acrobatic moves onto the table.
We make lists of what to talk about since the last time. Our grandchildren prefer
iPhones to books. They spend hours rewarded with blurry eyes, while we
remember growing up through summers of movies and picnics and new teenage
freedom. Her father took her to New York to watch operas while mine took me
to city league baseball games with Cokes and hot dogs. Her niece and nephew
are now having children. My granddaughter wants to be a zoo-keeper when she
grows up. Or perhaps a teacher. Or a Disney character. Her grandson plays baseball,
football, karate. She goes to all of the events and tells me all the play-by-plays
while we drink our morning coffee through the phone. He is breathing better now.

They fixed the O2 tank. They are going out to dinner with family and friends.

Once she whispered to me that she does not know what she will do
when he is gone. I do not know what to say. I know she will not accept
what I offer. It is not my place. It is not a part of our friendship. Now.
I am lost in my tears and my prayers. We are silent. While she waits.

EVENSONG

A SYMPHONY IN RED
FOR KATHRYN

There weren't many nail shops in Battle Creek where I grew up
so my mother painted her own nails in the only two colors
Revlon or Maybelline sold, or at least the only colors I remember.
Red was her favorite, bright and bold, like Christmas tree lights.
And I grew up mesmerized by her hands. Those nails.
I watched her smoke cigarettes, just like Betty Grable and Liz Taylor.
How she held her whiskey glass just-so. Or dabbed her lipstick.
How her hands moved when she spoke, especially in Italian.
The hands that wrapped my hair in curlers when I was three,
and four, and five. The hands that picked out the snazziest clothes
when we went shopping. The hands that buttoned me up
in chiffon dresses. Her nails, long and red, coaxing her brown hair
into a page-boy as I watched her in front of the mirror. Her hands
planting Tiger Lilies each summer in the backyard, and tucking
the tulip bulbs into the back of the kitchen cupboard each fall.
Her handwriting was like vermillion concertos, wafting across the stationery
in letters to family in Italy. Or even in notes to the milkman
to "leave cottage cheese next time."

I watched my mother's hands for four days after she died, waiting
for the rosary beads to move through her fingers. I memorized the wrinkles
that held memories she would take with her, people and places
from her childhood that she touched that I would never know.
Her hands that held jump ropes and salami sandwiches, notes passed in school,
held her giggles on her first date. The hands that held her tears when she miscarried
her first two babies. These hands. Swearing in Italian, swirling up the air
in a fortissimo of soundless motions. These hands. Now silent.
An echo. of the last note. of her.

WHEN I TOLD HOWARD MCCORD
I WAS MOVING TO MIAMI

For Howard McCord, RIP

he told me not to write poems about old people.
I wasn't old then, so I told him not to worry. I only write
about the dark voices inside me. About trees and winter nights.
The Michigan silence so loud I could never sleep. But there wasn't
any darkness in Florida. The nights light up like a carnival of stars
and white clouds. Each night I went outside to look up into the emptiness
of the skies because I had lost the darkness. The place where there are words.

So, Howard McCord reminded me not to write about old people.
And I said I wouldn't. But I told him they were everywhere,
with sagging breasts and bellies wrapped in beach blankets.
Or each other. Right there in the sand.
There were Botox and plastic surgery signs in doctor's offices, dental offices,
on bus stop benches. I saw a couple whose faces were stretched
and pulled tight with twisted noses, and cheek bones puffed up like balloons.
Tiny, swollen eyes. Big lips. There must have been a two-for-one
special-spectacle somewhere. And the funerals. Every day a new one.
Trails of Buicks driven into cemeteries by old people who lost a friend,
a wife, or husband. Maybe no one. They just go to funerals like my
grandmother used to do for something to do.
I saw a mausoleum in a cemetery with a plaque near the door
"I Told You I Was Sick." And another grave for a man buried
with his Cadillac. But I didn't write about them.

Twenty years later, I wrote to Howard McCord and told him
that I just wanted to write about anything, and he told me
not to write about old people because it was "cliché" and boring.
But I told him about the woman on the bus who dropped a dime.
I picked it up for her and she spit at me with "why do you have to be
so nice?" Everyone stared at me, shaking pin-curled or pink
or blue dyed hair, or black-dyed bald heads. I told him about
the old man who died in the grocery store, pushing his matted-fur dog,
keeling over in the vegetable section. I told him about the woman with
a red-wool scarf over her head who walks down my street. Staring. Stopping.
For hours. I told him about the once-Amish-woman who asks me every day
if I know how old the young women are who work for the Noah's Ark exhibit
in Kentucky, and if they are virgins.

After thirty years, I wrote to Howard McCord and said I was still trying to write.
He asked me who I was and told me maybe I should write about old people.
No one does that anymore.

36

A POEM FOR BRIGIT HOPE ON HER SIXTEENTH BIRTHDAY

For Monica

There is no sound,
the breath of each moment as silent as a prayer
without words or music.
She would live for two hours, still and quiet.
Without pain. Without cries.
And her mother will watch
as her last breath fills the room,
the sweet smell of life. and death.
She cannot not live here,
outside the womb that has bathed her
in darkness, caressed her with the echoes
of her mother's lullabies.
She will not live here,
this child who is daughter, miracle, hope
carried for nine months to have. These moments.
She does not open her eyes.
We want to believe. She will remember.

ODE TO A STONE: WHAT GOETHE COULD NOT KNOW

I faintly hear your voice, now,
thin threads of music like wind
in the tops of trees, drifting from leaf to leaf,
a river weaving through the darkness
inside you, twisting and turning over and over
like a woman braiding her hair or a song
dying and being reborn.

I hold you, touching the scars on your body
like an old poet discovering the soul of a poem.
In your womb you hide ancient stories, words
I do not know. I close my hand and feel the rhythm
rhythm of the moon inside you.

A PORTRAIT IN CRAYON

If I am very quiet, I can hear her, singing from her tree branch,
the smallest notes a crayon bird would warble behind its glass window.
It's my daughter's bird from second grade art class,
its yellowed beak now faded, its black talons still clinging
to a brown branch. It looks like a zoomed-in photograph because
she drew no tree, only that one large branch and a green leaf
which sits taller than this blue bird with its blue eye and its blue sky.
"The teacher said I had to fill in the whole paper," she told me.
The then-father scoffing, "You can't see the bird.
The whole background is blue. Stupid."
I hugged her and hung it on the wall.

Little bird, only one wing held up in the air, has journeyed with me
for forty years. She is old and faded. Crayon blues, yellows, browns
peeling in places, and water stains drip down the paper from a hurricane
that leaked down the wall. But, she is my daughter, tears streaking down
her face when kids at school called her Miss Piggy, the silent daughter
who kept secrets I never knew. The child who tried to hide,
like this little bird inside the huge blue background, so no one could see her,
no one could touch her again and leave invisible scars.
The little bird trying to fly away with one small wing, ever-watching
with one blue eye. "I know," I think each time I look at her. "I
remember."

THE GIFT

The sweet-smelling flowers lasted over a week in the vase. White Lily petals
were now dried and wrinkled beside the red roses that withered
over the edges of the bowl. Today they will join the garbage in the plastic bag.
The burial of something once alive, chopped and shipped to grocery stores
and flower shops across the country.
The only thing left is the red heart mylar balloon which had sent my dog
into hysteria and laryngitis for three days as it bobbed around over the table,
catching the sunlight from the windows, or an occasional breeze.
We are not allowed to send balloons into the sky. Something about
being harmful to marine life and causing pollution problems.
I do not know how far a little balloon can travel, and I do not
live near an ocean. I would not want to contribute to the death of anything,
even my poor, limp flowers ending up in the trash. But a heart balloon.
Something sacred, I think.
I let it go into the cloud jumbled sky and watched it for as long as I could.
It twisted and wiggled and swayed, dipping and diving, floating away
to someone else, I think. Someone who isn't loved, I hoped.
Someone who is alone and empty. A prayer, I whispered.

THE LAST MOMENTS
BEFORE SLEEP

I am constantly writing.
Even when my eyes are closed
I see words twisting like tornadoes.
There is someone in my head who is typing it all out
letter after letter.
The words, the images I forget and then remember,
but then are lost.
I am dressing myself with rhymes and songs
and I am floating in a sea of black water,
catching images of letters and notes
that look like fish flying
out and over the cloudless sky.
My boat is full of voices, twisting and twirling
in and out of my nakedness.
I am bending the night into another poem.

WHEN ABORTION WAS

You might have seen me that year playing and singing protests songs
strumming my Goya at rallies in Flint, Michigan, to stop Roe v. Wade.
You might have seen my bumper sticker "Abortion is Murder"
on the back of my shiny, white Impala.
It was 1971, when I was a good Catholic and a virgin.
We were a group of protestors, following the Pope
and all the beliefs we were told to believe, infiltrating meetings,
relentless and loud from the first argument and the second argument
before the Supreme Court put into law that a woman had the right to choose.

In 1973, my first child was born 13 days before it was legal to end the life
of a fetus. An embryo. A not-yet-baby. A mistake. I was twenty-four years old
and had no clue about motherhood, marriage. When my mother died,
I was twenty-one and had never had a date, a boyfriend, sex. I had spent
two of my years in the convent, learning to be quiet and holy and without sin.
When I was twenty-four I had a marriage, a divorce, a baby, and lived in a trailer.
I had gone from middle class to "barefoot and pregnant." But I loved my daughter
and worried that I could not take care of her. I tried to find a way to give her up
for adoption, so that she could eat something besides Spaghetti-O's. And cereal.
So she could have a mother and a father. Not just a mother who was afraid
to be one.

And then I wasn't. I moved. Refused welfare. I got a job. I paid rent. I bought groceries
and toys. For years, I did all the right things. I paid bills. I took my daughter to county
fairs and when she wanted to learn to ride a horse, I let her. We went to church,
every Sunday. And I prayed to be a good mother. A good Catholic. A good woman.

It was 1976, The Supreme Court had passed Roe v. Wade,
and Planned Parenthoods popped up in every city. I had stomach pain.
Like the flu. I went to the emergency room where the doctors said
they had to take x-rays and my blood. They never asked me if I might be pregnant.
Just gave me pills for pain. They found nothing. They sent me home.
And I took all the pills. The pain still there. I knew.
I cried that the pills had harmed it.
Planned Parenthood could not help me. with that.

We were careful. Oh my God, we were careful.
I could not have another child to care for. Alone.

I remembered the story in the church bulletin I read when I was in high school.
It was the story by an unborn child, excited to see her toes and fingers, excited
to hear her heart beat and her mother's voice. Until she wasn't. "Today, my mommy
is going to kill me."

It was 1976. No ultrasounds, No MRI's. Only the paper in my hand on my return visit
that read "No body parts found." The posters of tiny feet, tiny toes glared at me.
"This is what a 10-week-old fetus looks like" it read. But it made no difference.
What I had done.

I went home, and sang my daughter to sleep,
bleeding through the emptiness of my prayers.

WEAVING A POEM

I read them now, these poems of poets, who are dead and buried, whose hands bled words onto paper, grasped for phrases, cigarettes, lovers, Kerouac, Burroughs, Ginsberg, filling up coffee houses in low lights and each other, while I was trapped in the literature books of ridiculous rhymes, meeting Frost each year at the "Road Less Traveled". I could have been Bohemian instead of Italian, which probably would have suited my mother. The two of us, with a new generation to terrify my father's mother, hanging out in black tights and clicking fingers to the beat of the Beat on the street.

I did not read as a young girl. There were no books stuffed into the spaces of my summers, no words for me to find, one day, under my bed or in a drawer. I didn't know you then, dead poets, when I could have, all of you there in Michigan, writing, drinking, hording the nights with the words of Ginsberg's "Howl," Sinclair's raspy voice bellowing poems across the city, Hall and Kenyon making love and poems in his Ann Arbor apartment where his classes met before he was famous, all while I was a teenager and lost in a pit of religiosity, contemplating puberty and sin.

I could have tramped around, sang out, rallied, shouted, slashed my words into walls, sidewalks, and empty doorways in protest of war, racism, conformity, hatred. I could have wrapped myself up in the jazz of Clifford Brown's lyrical trumpet in Detroit and watched Philip Levine pulled into that penetrating cadence of his own words. I could have wrapped myself up in the terror of birth and death beside Roethke, weaving a poem to sing through my darkness.

THE PASSIONATE LADY
TO HER LOVE

For Steven

If you ask me, I will tell you
that I would rather wander through the crunch of a meadow
than hide my darkness inside silk and linen.
The smell of autumn pulls me further into the beauty of God
than sun beating down on my face.
I would make love to you here, nestled into the tall stalks
where corn grew all summer, rather than the senselessness
of white sheets, wrinkled into silence.
If Marlow were here, he would lead us to the fields
where sheep graze lazily, and we would picnic along the river
and discover its secrets made by the gentle breezes of September.
I would be your love and you'd be mine, and we would write our names
on the summer-bleached rocks on the hillside and whisper our desires
to the sunflowers woven into the orange sky of evening.
If you were to ask me, I would gather the songs of all the birds
to sing you to sleep in the chilling air, embroidered then
into a blanket of rhymes to keep us sheltered from any harm.

PRAYER

"AND WHEN THE LORD SAW HER,
HE HAD COMPASSION ON HER"
BUT HE DID NOT SAY TO HER,
"DO NOT WEEP. HERE'S A KLEENEX."

For Phyllis & Ted

I think if I were crying
Jesus would give me the corner of his robe
to dry my tears. He would not pull out a wade of tissues
from a cardboard box to soak up my sadness
and then throw it away. He would carry my sadness with Him,
let it dry into the cloth where His hands rested as He prayed,
touched the illnesses that He healed, His robes that held
the laughter of the children He loved.

I think if I were crying Jesus would take my tears with Him
on His journeys, letting them stain His fingers as He blessed
the poor and anointed the dying, and sang and prayed,
and pet goats and sheep, as He wandered over hills and valleys.

I think if I were crying, Jesus would wrap me up and hold my sadness
where He holds His own.

*Taken from Luke 7:13 (sort of)

WHAT DID MY FATHER THINK I WOULD DO WITH EDGAR A. GUEST'S 1928 POEMS?

When I hold the book of poetry, I remember things.
My father gave this to me when I was ten, and I never found out
how he got it. It was old then, pages already stained with age.
The smell of old people wafting out, the rhymes whispering out
about things old people do. Or did then. Especially in Michigan,
an odd place to be born, where I was born, just in time to see
women in house dresses and shoes that tied up. Purses always filled
with handkerchiefs and, a piece of candy or two, and foul-smelling oils.

I was a child on the brink of old-fashioned. Houses had wall paper, the kind
with little flowers and yellowed-out colors, and heat came up from the basement
through vents in the floors, and there were rugs in every room, rugs
on top of rugs that were vacuumed every week with the first Hoover
that swallowed up every sound in the entire house. My grandmother wore hair nets
and a brassiere with a girdle attached that fell down to her legs and had hooks
at the bottom for nylons that had dark lines crawling up the back. Her wrinkled up
breasts always reminded me of prunes. I would stare at mine later, taking them
out of my size A cups, and pray I would not have a onesie someday like hers.

I remember things when I hold this book. How the rhythm of long afternoons
and rivers and trees and row boats and fishing rods dripped into setting suns
on the pages, and, how he, this poet, had sailed into the stillness of his thoughts.
I can touch them when I touch this book: the children playing hide-and-seek,
catching fireflies and wishes in Mason jars.

WHEN I WAS FIFTEEN YEARS OLD

For Father Jim Bettendorf, R.I.P

I wanted to die.
I prayed for it daily, begged St. Therese to ask God to let it happen.
I waited, each day, for death to wrap me up and take me away.
I knew if I grew older, my holiness would drip off me
like the sun in the middle of July. I was no saint. I didn't want that.
I just wanted to die at my holiness peak.
In the summer I went to church every day with Cindy Loser
and we prayed for the repose of everyone's soul.
We put pebbles in our shoes to suffer for those souls in Purgatory.
The nuns told us we had to suffer to get into Heaven.
We doused ourselves in holy water and acts of contrition.

When I was fifteen years old, I read St. Therese's autobiography
for the first time wishing I had sisters like hers who all went into the convent
and never spoke another word except in silence before God.
Sisters who were pure and whose eyes reflected Heaven.
I didn't want to be a saint. I just wanted to be in love with God
and taken someplace where I could smell candles burning
and musty prayers would whisper through my virgin soul.

When I was fifteen, I wanted to be a nun. A nurse-nun.
I volunteered at Leila Hospital and worked with sick children.
Gloria was there, dying of leukemia. Her parents told me she had accepted death.
I didn't know what that meant. She was only twelve.
I watched her every afternoon, praying with her family. When she died,
the hospital room looked like any other. Nothing left. Of her. Or prayers.

At fifteen, I did my homework and took out the garbage.
I played with my dog and chewed my fingernails. I listened to the soap-opera
of my parent's fights. I wrote poems about lovely things I never saw.
I went to church and joined the Sunday choir. I went to confession
every week for sins I did not commit. And some that I did.

I read St. Therese's autobiography over and over
touching the worn-out pages as carefully as possible
hoping that her holiness would slip through my hands to my soul.
I didn't want to be a saint. When I was fifteen, I was confused about
so many things, except that I knew if lived any longer, I might die.

THE SILENCE OF THE DANCE

I have always watched the stars. Even when I was five years old
I would sit out in the backyard with my father as he pointed to each one.
I watched them with my own eyes
the way they dipped and slid across the black sky,
the quietness of their singing in and out of diaphanous clouds.

I would whisper secrets no one else could hear. Tell them stories
of what it's like to have the voices beating inside my head, wishes
that I could be with them, up there, where no one would find me.
My parents too consumed with hate for each other to know. Where I was.
That I was.

On those autumn nights, my father taught me their names,
names that I wove into wordless prayers, hoping they would hear.
Stars. They dance, you know. If you watch them long enough. And wait.

BACKGROUND MUSIC FOR A FUNERAL

For Barbara and her Country Man

1.
It only lasted a moment:
the flight of a lone eagle across a winter's sunset.

2.
Fog curls up in the hounds' ears.
They sniff at the air, remembering rabbits
hiding in the barren woods.

3.
Deer meander through the withered corn stalks
along these quiet country roads.
What you shared, you shared with no one else,
a lifetime now between you.

4.
Your memories circle the darkening sky.
Withering flowers press across
the shadows of your footsteps.

5.
Snow falls:
memories and dreams whisper
when eyes are closed.

AS THE DARK NIGHT WHISPERS
TO THE OCEAN

I will not venture into her singing
that begins as moonlight touches her dark blue body,
caresses her languid breath, and slips inside her womb
now empty and still. I watch from the shore, wishing myself
to enter the first wave of night, cleanse my nakedness of its sins.
But I am not of the sea, and I would drown in the dark song
that weaves itself in and out of my deepest yearnings, there
as it dances across the starlit waves, the melody of death
pulsing into my sleeping, its laughter teasing me to come to her.
I hear the echoes of prayers I have long forgotten in the rhythm
of waves splashing over the evening's mist. I sit and listen
to the music of water, sinking into the sand.

IN THE SUNRISE OF A
KEY WEST POEM

As I walk into this morning,
white-washed breezes
bring the smell of Old Town Bakery to me
as women pedal passed
on their squeaky bikes
with French loaves stuffed in their baskets.
Children run beside their mothers and giggle,
warm buns squished in their hands.

The air, still cool from evening winds,
brings echoes of blue-green sea
that wafts through my skin
like a water-colored painting
while I think of old poets, miles away,
opening book after book of their writings
searching for themselves in the yellowing words.

I stop to pet a cat or two,
stretched out on someone's wooden porch
or along the cracked up-turned sidewalks.
Night has undressed itself and it is a morning of pelicans
and weather-worn fishing boats, and I will wander to the shore
and into the sea foam, picking up sun-bleached shells
with my bare toes, my footprints disappearing into the sand.
Today I am a seagull.

WHAT MY GRANDMOTHER TOLD ME AFTER SHE DIED

I remember the dream, where I woke up inside of it,
Into the grayness of the sky. The morning in the dream
when my grandmother took preserves
from the pantry and spread them over my oatmeal
then bundled me up and led me to the fields
to hunt for milkweed pods.
My boots crushed the dried up branches,
the very touch of my fingers
scattering dust into my hair and eye lashes
while my grandmother made no noise, like a nun in prayer,
secreting into the dead garden, knowing which shells to pick
and lay into her soft brown apron.

For hours we painted the pods in blues and yellows and reds
then dressed them in scraps of cloth, and they looked
like little old ladies holding babushkas over their wrinkled faces.
In my dream we strung them in rows to hang from the kitchen windows
where they danced against the cold glass, as my grandmother
sang songs with words I did not know and I woke up alone
to the sunlight piercing the morning. "They are praying,"
she had whispered. "Your soul can sing, you know."

THE ANOINTING OF ANNA GRACE

For Anna

My granddaughter works at a park each Saturday.
It was her choice to become a volunteer.
Even on the first day I wasn't completely convinced
this selflessness would last past an hour.
Her first task was to shovel horse poop out of the petting zoo,
and without a grimace, wearing her most expensive Pumba's,
she took the shovel and gloves and scooped. And scooped,
later hosing down the ponies, laughing with other girls she did not know.

I visit each Saturday, and watch as she chases Hazel,
the 200-pound-pig with the nasty attitude, away from the little kids
who come into the petting zoo to giggle at the goat and pet the ponies.
Now wearing her Wellies, she rakes and soaps and sprays,
walks children around on the ponies, and has conversations with parents
about Jimmy, the donkey, who knows how to open the gates,
so that all the animals can escape. "So please be careful leaving
or he will go with you."

Once I saw Hazel sneaking up on her, ready to bite her foot,
and then my granddaughter shaking her finger at this enormous,
smelly, pot-bellied animal while she scooted around,
dodging chickens and roosters who flew up in her face,
her arms and hands twirling in the air, her lips pressed in authority.
And all the squawks and grunts filled up the air in a musical charade
to this 4'11" 's commands. "Hazel, don't even think about it!"

A TALE OF TWO IN THREE PARTS

I never wanted to be a teacher.
I avoided the subject whenever I could
and found it strange that my second husband
and his mother, his two brothers and their wives
had taught school for a hundred years.
I was content working as a secretary and writing poems
and raising my daughter in the foreign land of Miami
where coconuts flew around in the deluge of rainstorms,
people in Overtown burned down their own homes and businesses,
and sharks migrated into beach waters.
I never wanted to be a teacher until I needed a job
and the only one available was as a substitute,
arguing the theme of resurrection in *A Tale of Two Cities*
in a class of tenth graders. I didn't know Billy then,
a history teacher, famous for his student-field trips to Washington, D.C.
and his swaggering attitude of ties and polished shoes. Always pristine.
Always the attitude. On the second day of *A Tale of Two Cities*,
I decided that teaching was fun, and on the third day, I was permanently hired.
And on the fourth day, Billy informed me that there were no books,
there wasn't a syllabi, and my job was to keep the children content
so the parents would not complain. Billy was a showman, bound for success, a
know-it-all-Southern-accented-I'm-in-your-face-and-you'd better-listen-kind-of
guy. He thought I was the most unqualified applicant for the position.
I thought he was the most arrogant, annoying person I had ever met
and I prayed he didn't have a wife.

70

In 1984, America was introduced to the disease.

One had to be fearless to fight off all the quakes of information

that spread just as fast. The mysteries and the myths.

Ryan White, the first child introduced as a child with AIDS. The lies.

The pain and suffering he endured just to be a kid.

He was going to be a hero. He was going to fight for his rights

to be alive, and go to school, and not infect anyone.....ever.

And he was going to die, while the lies infected us more than AIDS.

The stories of exotic birds infecting tourists. How infected monkeys

spread this disease. Make a note: stay away from parrots and monkeys.

Don't touch. Don't kiss. Don't have sex. Don't drink from the same water

fountain. How the homosexuals caused the epidemic. Ok, so they hung out

with exotic birds and monkeys? I knew a lot of gay people. They were

my friends. We worked together. We hung out and partied together.

We talked about the epidemic. I hoped they would be safe.

Billy called me one night. He was sick and needed a ride to the ER.

He had no one to take him. He needed a doctor. I called mine,

who asked me, post examination, if Billy had been out of the country

or owned an exotic bird.

It was the first of many trips to the hospital. The first of many secrets kept.

He was dying, he said. Maybe there will be a cure soon enough, I said.

On a Saturday in April, 1984, I received a phone call
from Billy's best friend. Billy had 24-hours to live. Could I come
and say good-bye? I'd better come now. "He really wants you here."
The room was filled with gay men, all there to comfort him.
I was the only woman. The only heterosexual. The only fellow teacher.
I had never faced death this way....a-right-there-in-my-face, sort of thing.
I refused to wear the gown, the mask, the gloves. I sat on his bed
and held his hand. I held his eyes in mine. We held the silence together.
There would be no funeral. His parents were coming from Arkansas.
To take him away. I kissed him on the cheek.
"You shouldn't have done that," he whispered.
"Yes, I should have," I whispered back.

YOU CAN HIDE A LOT OF PRAYERS
IN A SOUL

When I left the convent
I went to parks and forests where rocks grew
and with ink and my pen, I wrote poems on them
and then painted them with nail polish
so they wouldn't disappear. I left them there
for people to read as they made love, or had picnics,
or slept on the benches, or watched dogs pee
and chase frisbees. People with tears and fears,
lonely and empty with no words to keep them warm.
The words poured out over my fingers
and they were sad and joyful and mixed together,
dripping prayers that I never had the chance to say
because I was told me I wasn't holy enough to be
in the stained-glass presence of mystical sainthood.
Here, in the scent of trees and rivers,
my soul can breathe the prayers God has created.
I hear them singing in the poems I leave behind.

I saw a tear in the rain
and it fell upon a stone
and the stone died

THE PHILLY CHEESE-STEAK SANDWICH

I lost another word yesterday. Right there in Flannigan's Pub.
We were eating dinner, laughing, commenting on how the waitress
wasn't wearing a mask, and I said to my husband, "This is the best…."
I looked at my plate, my food right there in front of me,
the bun, mayo, meat, cheese, my eyes staring down at my food.
Yes, it was food. I'd had it before. "What is this?" I asked.

I'm a poet, a grandmother, a wife. I talk and sing and dance
and bake cookies. For the first time in my whole life
I *have* a life. I no longer put my hands over my ears and hide
behind furniture because I am afraid my parents will kill each other.
I do not run down the street to call the police after my father leaves
my black-and-blue mother. I have a husband, puppies, and neighbors.
I teach school, and I crochet blankets. I read books. I pray
for the repose of the soul of everyone who has died or those who just need
one a prayer to hold onto. I'm losing my words and I am *afraid* I am losing my words.

Today, I named everything I saw, over and over and over again.
Paper, computer, pencil, tree, car, bushes, cell phone, door, book,
coffee cup, garbage pail. I told the birdfeeder it was a birdfeeder,
and the clock it was a clock, the door it was a door.
I even spoke to the bar of soap in the bathroom about being soap.
I am afraid I will die and go to heaven and not know I'm there.
I won't remember God, and will ask Him, "Who are you?"
I won't remember that I don't remember.
Today, I named everything I saw, over and over and over again.

"IT IS IMPORTANT TO KNOW WHERE YOU WERE PUT ON THE FACE OF THE EARTH"

—Thomas Merton

I grew up around sunflower fields.
The silence of the warm sun on September mornings
right after the darkness slips away
and the haze of sleep disappears.
The bobbing of round faces, and long leaves,
green and shiny.
Bees humming as they gather their nectar,
then fly away to hives nearby.

I thought I should have grown up on a farm or in a forest,
woods and pastures that would wrap around me
like the prayers of cloistered nuns, so loud
in their silence. When I was young, I hugged trees
and sang songs out loud. I looked for leaves or rocks, left
especially for me, I would pretend. I would open my arms wide
to the winter sun, so bright and cold, leave footprints
along the paths where trees sent white showers into my hair.
I followed pathways through the trees and bushes
near my home and pretended I lived in there
where I could talk to God. By myself.

I am beginning to be old. I still hug trees and sing out loud
whenever I want to. I sit outside and watch the wind
braid itself inside clouds while the sun walks slowly across the grass
as the shadows of birds and bees fingerprint the afternoons.
I plant sunflowers along my fence and collect shells and pebbles
from the ocean, sun bleached and left behind in the dancing
of the waves. And I sit on the shore, alone with the whispering silence
of the ocean's only song.

I am meant to be here in the glory of every breathing thing.

THE FINDING OF

It was the desperation of being an only child that brought me
to look for things. I loved things. Pennies dropped carelessly
on the sidewalk because they were pennies and not worth much.
Colorful beads that had fallen from someone's necklace or bracelet.
A pencil or pen or one earring. During the summers I was on my own
all day long while my mother worked or caroused with her friends
and my father slept from working the nightshift at Kelloggs.
My friends were vacationing or shopping with their parents, while I
was left to wander through the neighborhood. By myself.

There was a small grove of trees down the hill next to the old man's house
who owned a dog called "You Know." (When you asked him
what his dog's name was he would always say "you know.")
The old man had a shack-type house and wore the same clothes every day,
and I could always find him sitting in a chair in the middle of his grassless yard
with You Know. He threw away the most wonderous things in that tree grove.
I found cups, and spoons, and tarnished jewelry, but mostly whiskey bottles
whose glass rainbowed in the sun, yellows and reds and blues, in twisted
and swirly shapes. And I brought them home and put flowers in them.

Sometimes I walked the summer path all of us kids took to school,
up and over the hill that we could all see from our backyards. I walked slower,
head down, looking, waiting to find what was waiting for me to find.
There were flowers blooming, although my dad told me they were just weeds,
and I would whisper "thank you, God" before touching them.
Sometimes I found erasers or crayons, which I stuffed in my shorts' pockets.
Other times I'd see milkweeds opening to free the small angels that floated
from their wombs. Sometimes, keys or buttons. Sometimes the glimmer
of sunshine on newly born leaves or rocks in the shape of hearts,
which I would leave for someone else.

When I grew older, like 12, all my friends had moved away,
and I was the only one to walk to school. The old man had died
and a brand new house was built where that shack once stood
and the tree grove wasn't more than a tree grove.
I also watched a church being built across the street from my house,
in the field I looked for baby rabbits and left over toys around the
dilapidated home where a welfare woman lived with the children
she birthed every year. In a few months, the holy-rollers took up entire
Sundays, clapping their hands and yelling their prayers, while my father
watched football and drank beer or fought with my mother if she was home
and I played with my dolls inside the cloister of my bedroom.
Sometimes I thought God had snuck in because I could feel Him
sitting there on the bed, listening to me, watching me.
We didn't talk much about God in my house, so I kept Him a secret.
We didn't talk, He and I. I figured He needed the silence, too.

SACRED SPACE
—*Antonius Roberts*

Until today, I had only watched her from a distance
as she stood in her own shadow,
an almost song wrapping itself into the morning tide.

Until today, I had only sent my prayers
into the thin breeze that wrapped itself into the lapping of waves
while she stood alone, watching the wind singing
over the ocean.

She is silent in the loudest way, reaching upward, without arms
to touch the first colors of the sun, watching the dance
of sea foam as it spills over the sand.

I am beside her in a prayer, the rugged wood of her body
brushing against the wrinkles of my skin, the song
we have sung alone, rising above us into one voice.

Until today, I had never seen her heart, open and waiting,
the darkness dripping into the whisperings of our souls.

ALONE IN THE WOODS

Along the river that weaves itself through this forest,
bits of ice still cling to branches and water-soaked leaves.
It is not yet spring, but birds are building nests
and squirrels flick their tails, then scurry from branch to branch.
The early evening fog touches my face,
brushing me in its silence so loud I hear every. thing.
The trees smell sweet and cold as I lift my hand and hold
the last drops of the sun before they slip away.
The moon is a thin line, a shadow on the edge of my lips.
I whisper to the owls who are swooping out from their hollowed trees,
"Sometimes, it is necessary to *be* the prayer."

COMPLETORIUM

My daughter, Cathryn Leigh, wrote her poem when she was in
5th grade.
My granddaughter, Anna Grace, wrote her poem when she was in
the 8th grade.
Both are prayers in my life, as are the poems they have written.

THE LORD IS MY RAINBOW

He makes me smile.
Through yellow and orange He teaches me.
He gives me comfort in the blue and green.
He guides me over the arch.
Even though I walk through the dark clouds
I am not scared because He is next to me.
With His purple and red He gives me courage.

He places a pot of grace in front of me
so my enemies can see it.
He blesses me with sunshine and rain.
I am over-filled with joy.
Only promises of love will follow me
for the rest of my life.
I shall walk in God's colors for the rest of my years to come.

— Cathryn Leigh

MY NIGHTTIME GARDEN

My nighttime garden
is full of fireflies.
I can hear the wind whispering
in the clouds
and owls watching in the trees.

In my nighttime garden
I can splash my naked feet
in the pond
and look into the sky full of stars
shining like diamonds.

In my nighttime garden
every flower smells like a rainbow
and crickets chirp their songs
to the sleeping grass.
My nighttime garden is the place
I want to be alone.
— Anna Grace

ABOUT THE AUTHOR

Karyn M. Bruce is a graduate of Bowling Green State University with a BFA in Creative Writing. She holds a M.A. in Literature and an Ed.S. in Education from Barry University, Miami Shores, FL. For 18 years, she taught middle school English, and until it's closing in 2021, she was a freshman English professor at Johnson & Wales University, North Miami, Florida. She currently works at the Alternative Education Academy, teaching English and writing to children with learning difficulties.

Karyn is the author of two other books of poetry: *Through Every Season Bright and New* (1988) (out of print), and *I Will Write Loudly So You Can Hear Me (2018)*. She and her husband live in Miami, FL, with two cocker spaniels, Lillie Joel and Lucie Marie.